20ᵀᴴ CENTURY · DESIGN

THE 90s

THE DIGITAL AGE

20TH CENTURY DESIGN – The '90s
was produced by

David West ☆☆ Children's Books
7 Princeton Court
55 Felsham Road
London SW15 1AZ

Picture Research: Brooks Krikler Research
Editor: Clare Oliver
Additional research: Adam Hibbert

First published in Great Britain in 1999 by
Heinemann Library, Halley Court, Jordan Hill,
Oxford OX2 8EJ, a division of Reed Educational and
Professional Publishing Limited.

OXFORD MELBOURNE AUCKLAND
JOHANNESBURG BLANTYRE GABORONE
IBADAN PORTSMOUTH (NH) USA CHICAGO

Copyright © 1999 David West Children's Books

03 02 01 00 99
10 9 8 7 6 5 4 3 2 1

ISBN 0 431 03960 7 (HB)
ISBN 0 431 03961 5 (PB)

British Library Cataloguing in Publication Data

Ford, Hannah
   al age (1990s). - (Design in the
twentieth century)
1. Design - History - 20th century - Juvenile literature
I. Title
745.4'442

Printed and bound in Italy

PHOTO CREDITS :
Abbreviations: t-top, m-middle, b-bottom,
r-right, l-left, c-centre.

Cover & 28t - Glaxo Wellcome. Cover tr,
4t, 5bl & br, 6br, 6-7, 12t,13tl & tr, 16br,
18bl, 20m & b, 21t & m, 22t, m & br,
23l, 26bl, 27tl & 29bm - Frank Spooner
Pictures. Cover ml, 16t, 17t & m & 19
all - Courtesy Ron Arad Associates.
Cover mr, 3, 5t, 7bm, 10-11 & 11tm -
Courtesy Apple Macintosh. Cover bl &
25tl - Renault. Cover bc & 24t -
Volkswagen. Cover br, 18br, 18-19 &
21b - AKG London. 4b & 27tr -
Mercedes Benz. 6bl - Sharp. 7br -
Vodafone. 8t & 9tr - Sony.
8m - Casio. 8b - National Westminster
Bank. 9m & 11tr - Philips. 12 - M.
Hutson/Redferns. 12br, 20t, 22bl & 23r -
Corbis. 13b - Arthur Elgort ©
Vogue/Condé Nast Publications Ltd. 15
both Inflate Ltd. 16m - Lara Grylls
P.R/Becca Russel. 16bl - Zanussi. 17b -
Ron Arad & Inflate Design Studio. 24m,
25tr & 27b - BMW. 24b - Solution
Pictures. 24-25 - Milepost 92 1/2. 25bl -
Castrol. 26t - Freeplay. 26br - Club Med.
28bl - Division Ltd. 28br - NASA. 29t -
Me Company. 29br - 1st Independent
(courtesy Kobal collection).

*The dates in brackets after a designer's
name give the years that he or she lived.
Where a date appears after an object (or, in
the case of a building, the town where it is
situated), it is the year of its design.
'C.' stands for circa, meaning about or
approximately.*

*An explanation of difficult words can be
found in the glossary on page 30.*

20TH CENTURY · DESIGN

THE 90s

THE DIGITAL AGE

Hannah Ford

Heinemann
LIBRARY

CONTENTS

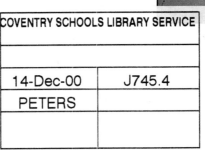
Models showed off combat-style fashion on the streets of New York during the Gulf War. The war was triggered by Iraq's invasion of Kuwait ('90). Throughout the decade the Western powers tried to remove Iraqi leader Saddam Hussein from power.

Ever-growing congestion brought cities to a standstill. Consumers finally accepted smaller cars, such as the Smart (above) and the Ka.

IT'S A SMALL WORLD

The 1990s began with a period of recession. Even after economic recovery, some felt that their working lives were less important and that the emphasis should be on lifestyle.

There was a reaction against the materialism of the 1980s, though any anti-fashion was soon picked up by the media and transformed into the height of chic. No-name brands, such as Muji, were ultra desirable, and Alessi's tongue-in-cheek designs sold thousands.

Computers became simpler to use, and were no longer just for whizz kids and geeks. The dawn of the internet revolutionised communications and the marketplace. Satellite, cable and digital TV brought the world closer. The decade began with 24-hour satellite news coverage of the Gulf War and ended with troubles in the Balkans, civil wars in Africa and border disputes in Asia.

As the 21st century dawns, no one knows what lies ahead but two things, at least, are certain: the pace of change is accelerating and the future will be what we make it.

Teleworking (working from home) became a reality in the '90s. The good-looking iMac was aimed at the home market.

Italian firm Alessi brought fun, friendly design into people's homes.

The Millennium Dome, London, was built as a showcase for new technologies and to usher in the 21st century.

The first virtual stars appeared. They were easier to control than real-life flesh-and-blood ones!

5

DIGITAL DECADE

By the end of the 1990s, digital technology was part of everyday life. Personal computers were in most homes and the World Wide Web followed them. Everything from the TV to the kitchen toaster was now run by microchips. Digital technology was the gold mine of the '90s, and amazing new products appeared every year.

DIGITAL DAWN

Digital technology was established in the 1960s, but until the '90s only big businesses and universities had benefitted from it. As computers became easier to use, and as microchips became faster, smaller and more reliable, digital technology became useful in everyday life. Items such as this book could now be made by a few people swapping files from computer to computer, and household objects such as video cameras became sophisticated number-crunchers.

The Nikon E2 digital camera was introduced in March '96. Photographs could now be passed straight to a computer, cutting out all that fiddly, expensive film processing.

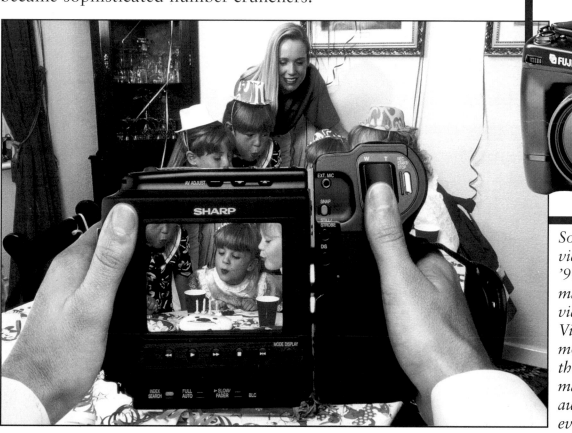

So many people owned video players by the '90s that there was a big market for easily-operated video cameras. This Sharp Viewcam used a flat screen, mounted independently of the lens, to give the film-maker freedom to hold it away from the eye – or even overhead in a crowd.

Making computers more user-friendly was vital as digital gadgets became more widely used. The screen of the Newton (*below*) allowed users to write by hand. The special pen presses two transparent wiring grids together, creating a tiny electrical charge. The computer 'feels' the pattern of charges, and works out which letter or number you have written. Charges in the grid make tiny LCDs below turn black, leaving the writing visible to you – in digital ink.

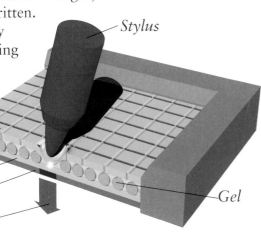

Stylus

Metal conductive sheet covered with protective layer

Metal conductive sheet

Miniature LCD layer

Information to processor

Gel

Digital technology brought computing and TV together. TV broadcasters went digital, to free up airspace for new channels, while computer resources such as the internet were made accessible from TV sets such as the Philips Web TV ('96).

THE END OF VIDEO?

1998 saw the arrival of a digital storage and retrieval system known as DVD, or Digital Versatile Disc. DVD was designed to cope with most of the different kinds of jobs previously done by separate machines – video players, games consoles and CD players. All these functions were together in one simple box.

   DVD's advantages over these older gadgets were due to its digital technology. It was now possible to skip to a favourite part of a film without having to wind a tape backwards and forwards. DVD discs would last a lot longer than magnetic tape as well – they wouldn't go fuzzy as they grew old.

7

DIGITAL VS. ANALOGUE

Digital gadgets use a code of On and Off (1 and 0) to carry and process information. Analogue systems use changes in the strength of a signal to reproduce information. Digital technologies mostly replaced old analogue ones in the '90s because digital systems tend to be quicker, cheaper, more reliable and more portable. Some people still believe that analogue provides better quality, preferring music on vinyl records to CDs.

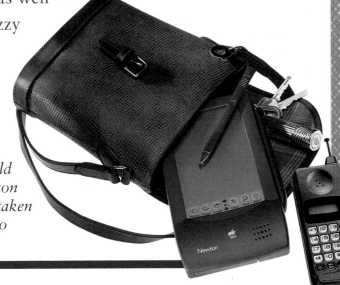

Pocket-sized computers such as the Apple Newton ('93) appeared. Hand-written notes could be faxed from the Newton via a mobile phone, or taken home to download on to a word processor.

MICRO GADGETRY

With the mass production of microchips came a new generation of micro gadgets – it was suddenly possible to fit a whole weather station on to a wristwatch, a perfect navigator into your pocket, or a collection of your top 1,000 pop tunes in the palm of your hand!

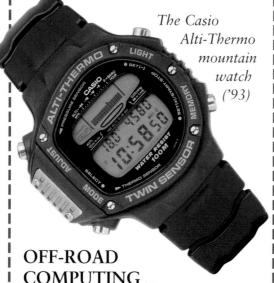

The Casio Alti-Thermo mountain watch ('93)

OFF-ROAD COMPUTING

Entirely new products appeared with the availability of cheap microchips. This Casio wristwatch, designed for mountaineers and skiers, contained two sensors, to read air pressure and temperature. The watch's microchip guessed at height above sea level from changes in air pressure.

MORE JUICY

As greater numbers of people were able to afford quite sophisticated electronic gadgets, demand for smaller and more stylish designs grew. Mobile phones shrank from the size and weight of a hefty briefcase to slimline pocket phones that could easily be taken everywhere. Designs progressed from ugly black bricks to shiny, curvy lifestyle accessories in a rainbow of colours.

The Sony Pyxis handheld Global Positioning System gave explorers and hikers perfect map-reading ability. It compared tiny delays from three satellite signals, and calculated its position to within a few metres.

With Mondex ('90) it became possible to carry your bank around in your pocket. Mondex cards store 'electronic cash' on a chip, which can be read by a key fob. A 'wallet' allows card-holders to make transactions that would previously have required a time-consuming trip to the nearest bank.

FIGHTING FOR THE FUTURE

Digital gave manufacturers with imagination the chance to make new markets, for example by inventing the GPS. But sometimes new products clashed and companies had to jockey for position in the digital future.

In the search for the smallest of everything, manufacturers occasionally missed the mark. Few people wanted to watch television whilst out jogging.

The Philips Digital Compact Cassette ('92) was meant to replace old-fashioned tapes. But clever design failed to ensure success in the market.

OUT WITH THE OLD

Digital recordings had conquered the music industry by the 1990s, with the compact disc. Tape recorders began to seem too bulky and slow, and two possible replacements emerged: MiniDisc and DCC, a digital tape. Each one had its advantages, though as with VHS and BetaMax video formats in the '80s, only one could survive. As the two formats battled it out, the future arrived in the shape of MP3 ('98). Music could now be downloaded from the internet on to a chip, and played at CD-quality for hours.

THE MAGIC OF MINIDISCS

The Sony MiniDisc ('92) was designed to be used for making recordings at home and on the move. CDs are made by burning holes into metal foil with a laser. This makes a recording that can never be changed. Sony had to invent a new system to make the MiniDisc re-recordable. The MiniDisc recording heads combine two very different technologies.

First, a laser beam is used to soften the metal in a tiny spot. Second, a magnetic head swipes the hot spot, leaving a pattern of magnetised metal. When a special polarised light is bounced off the surface, the magnetic spots cause the beam to change very slightly. The change is just strong enough for the disc player to decode as music.

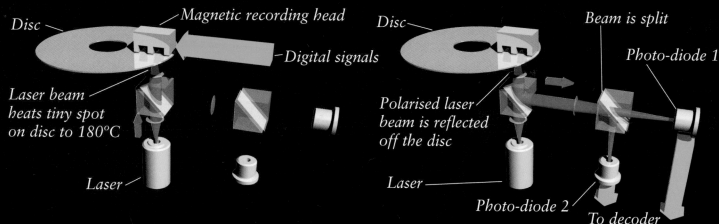

Disc — Magnetic recording head
— Digital signals
Laser beam heats tiny spot on disc to 180°C
Laser

Disc — Beam is split
Photo-diode 1
Polarised laser beam is reflected off the disc
Laser
Photo-diode 2
To decoder

COOL COMPUTERS

Before the 1990s, computers were rarely seen outside big offices, factories and universities. But as they became cheaper and more widely-used, people began to want them in the home. Some were used for working at home – but they were also great for playing games!

The Nintendo GameBoy enjoyed a revival in the late '90s when it was rebuilt with trendy new plastics.

OFFICE BORE

Apart from their cost, the problem for domestic consumers was that the machines looked like ugly square lumps of office furniture. Ever since the early days of office machinery, when the United States Army was one of the world's biggest buyers, computers had been made in army regulation beige. Now that people wanted to have them in their homes, designers had to rethink. Apple led the way in the late 1990s with a new range of fun and colourful computers for the home or office. Using a computer felt more like playing than ever before!

Sony's PlayStation ('96) brought more computer power to video gaming than it took to put man on the Moon in '69.

POCKET PETS

Designers trying to make computers more friendly realised that they could give them a cute personality. In '97, there was a craze around the world for Bandai's Tamagotchi, an egg-shaped toy containing a virtual pet on a microchip. If the pet wasn't cared for properly, it could become a little monster, and even die!

Tamagotchi was the size of a keyring.

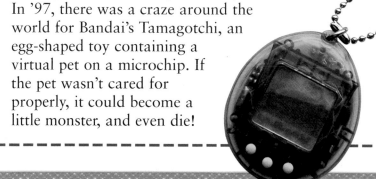

The Apple iMac ('98) was designed to make it fun to have in the home. The translucent colours of the plastic were borrowed from boiled sweets.

The Apple eMate ('97) was made for schools. Its light but tough shell made it ideal for withstanding rough treatment from children.

Computers were also used to teach at home. This interactive Philips system taught basic maths and reading skills.

WIRED WORLD

The most important part of the computer revolution was the World Wide Web. The internet used to be hard to understand, and was used mainly by scientists until 1993, when the release of a new and simpler computer code made the World Wide Web possible. The internet boom began. By '98, it was an important part of the world economy, and 'surfing' was a cool new hobby. Home-users made sure that there was plenty of art, music and gaming to be enjoyed, alongside the practical stuff.

GETTING CONNECTED

With computers and their accessories becoming cheaper, many people had access to the World Wide Web. Some home-users now had scanners, digital cameras and CD-drives for loading music and pictures. These could be sent over a modem to a website, which other people, anywhere in the world, could access. Downloaded files could be saved to a hard drive, printed out, played over speakers, or recorded on to a CD or removable disc.

Speakers

Digital camera

Printer

CPU

Monitor

Digital information to and from internet

Removable hard disc

Mouse

Keyboard

CD

Scanner

FASHION

The 1990s saw a reaction against the showy power suits of the '80s. Post-modern designers plundered the past, reviving styles of the '40s, '50s, '60s and '70s. And they looked to popular culture for fresh ideas. Sportswear and dance culture provided rich sources of inspiration.

RISE TO THE CHALLENGE

More and more, people used fashion as a way to express their beliefs and present challenging ideas. After rising to fame in the 1970s and '80s as the 'mother of punk', British designer Vivienne Westwood (b.1941) continued to bring out shocking, irreverent collections. She cleverly mixed visual motifs of the past and present.

For Vive la Cocotte ('95) she revived 18th-century ballgowns; her Anglomania range ('93) fused denim streetwear with oriental motifs.

Animal prints had numerous revivals during the '90s. In line with concerns for wildlife, high-fashion furs were fake, not real.

12

Westwood is famed for her outrageous creations, such as this ballgown ('95). She took historical styles – that once imprisoned women – and reclaimed them.

WESTWOOD'S LEGACY

Punk fashions of the '70s were updated. Dressed in leather and plastic, androgynous cyberpunks seemed to have stepped off the set of a science-fiction film. For a post-apocalypse look, they mixed 'found' objects with rubber and metal fabrics.

Metal tea-strainers made perfect cyberpunk goggles!

BRAVING THE ELEMENTS

The '80s saw the advent of an important new fashion trend, as clothes and materials developed for sports crossed over into mainstream fashion. DuPont's Lycra was followed by new synthetics such as Tencel, Polartec and Gore-Tex. Windproof, waterproof and 'breathable', Gore-Tex was no longer worn only by skiers and snowboarders. It was used by Nike to cover their state-of-the-art running shoes and by US designer Ralph Lauren (*b*.1939) for his label RLX, introduced in Autumn '99.

Windproof: outer shell deflects wind

Gore-Tex is ideal for sportswear. It keeps out the elements but allows perspiration to evaporate.

Outer shell

Waterproof: each pore is 20,000 times smaller than a raindrop

Breathable: micropores allow body moisture to escape

Inner shell

Skirt-wearing French couturier Jean-Paul Gaultier liked to challenge people's preconceptions about sexuality.

French designer Jean-Paul Gaultier (*b*.1952) was also out to shock. In the late 1980s and early '90s he championed underwear as outerwear, when he dressed Madonna in glitzy, jewel-encrusted corsets for her 'Blonde Ambition' tour.

ANTI FASHION

Casual clothes – stretchy leggings and comfortable trainers – slowly became wardrobe staples. Nike, Adidas and Reebok were soon household names. Diesel, Firetrap and other streetwise brands used high-tech fabrics for their laid-back designs, and before long top designers copied the sporty look.

Haute couture met sportswear in these high-fashion Chanel trainers ('97). The V-neck is by Escada Sport.

13

FUN & STYLE IN THE HOME

In the post-modern (or after modernism) age, many designers consider an object's form first, sometimes at the expense of its performance.

GioStyle's Flori range in candy-coloured plastic includes a jolly juicer and a multi-purpose storage bin.

USEFUL VS. PLAYFUL

This is in contrast to the modernists. The German architect Mies van der Rohe (1886–1969) summed up modernism with the phrase 'form follows function'. One humorous and post-modern response to this was to relate products to their function in a cartoonish way. This was seen in colanders shaped like lettuce leaves, and in much of the Alessi range, which included Coccodandy (an egg-boiler with a handle shaped like a hen) and plastic spice pots whose lids were decorated with models of their contents (nutmeg, chilli or basil).

Philippe Starck's leggy Juicy Salif lemon squeezer ('90) was beautiful to look at and sold extremely well. A glass was placed inside the legs and the juice would run down into it.

SHOWCASE DESIGN

Objects that were once barely noticed, such as toilet brushes, bins and lemon squeezers, were now designed for display. In fact, the stylish Juicy Salif lemon squeezer, with its science-fiction silhouette, was too tall to fit into most cupboards!

In a witty take on the modernists' 'form follows function', this colander resembles the salad leaves that it is used to drain!

HOLLOW PLASTIC

The newest plastic objects looked good enough to eat and were made in the same way as Easter eggs! A drop of liquid plastic was poured into half of the mould (1). The other half of the mould enclosed the plastic (2). Then the mould was gently rocked (3) so that the whole inside surface was thinly coated with the liquid plastic.

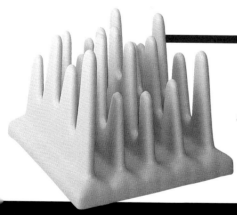

Set up in '95, British firm Inflate used PVC for its playful products, such as this inflatable fruit bowl.

The little devil bottle-opener ('94) was designed by Biagio Cisotti for Alessi.

NEO-POP

Many designers returned to the pop art of the 1960s for inspiration. Sleek metal was replaced by bright, kindergarten colours. Plastic, one of the cheapest, most versatile materials around, became more popular than ever. Inflate (*f.*1995) used dip-moulded PVC to create blow-up items for the home ranging from chairs to fruit bowls! And even 'hard' modern plastics were matt-finished, translucent and soft to the touch.

Inflate's Digital Grass was as suitable for the home office as for the kitchen – it could be a toast or letter rack!

This technique allowed designers to create plastic objects that were completely smooth, with no joins or rough edges.

1
2
3
4

ALESSI

In '93 the Italian manufacturers Alessi introduced their Family Follows Fiction (FFF) range, which used a mixture of polyamide (a type of plastic) and stainless steel. The 'family' included a sugar sifter called Gino Zucchino, a bottle cap called Carlo, glass storage jars called Gianni and a plastic biscuit box called Mary, which oozed a delicious biscuity smell. Key to the Alessi range was the idea of giving the products friendly names, to encourage a relationship between the object and user. The use of bright, colourful plastic gave the range toy-like appeal, and Alessi managed to subvert the notion of plastic being 'cheap' by making the range expensive and exclusive.

The full name for the humorous Alessi storage jar was 'Gianni, a little man holding on tight'!

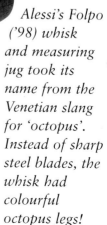

Designed by Alessandro Mendini, the Anna G corkscrew ('94) spawned a whole host of Anna G products.

Alessi's Folpo ('98) whisk and measuring jug took its name from the Venetian slang for 'octopus'. Instead of sharp steel blades, the whisk had colourful octopus legs!

CURVY FORMS

Like product designers, furniture makers increasingly reverted to the soft, curvy forms of the 1960s. Organic chairs, tables and shelves inhabited people's homes like familiar friends, but the designers used man-made materials (such as plastic, glass and steel) and non-natural colours to emphasise that these objects were created – and not organic at all.

For his Fantastic Plastic Elastic chair ('97), Ron Arad combined ultra-modern materials – see-through plastic on a tubular aluminium frame – to create a curvy effect.

This elegant, simple glass chair by Becca Russel ('99) consisted of four sheets of bent glass bolted together.

COOL FRIENDS

Kitchen appliances are sometimes called white goods, because they usually come in white enamel. But in the '90s some designers replaced white boxes with organic forms. Swedish company Zanussi gave their products soft, rounded feet and identified them by friendly names instead of numbers. The prototype Zoe washing machine ('99) was really lovable – she could decide which washing cycle to run.

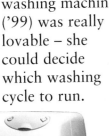

Zoe washing machine   Oz refrigerator ('98)

Designers enjoy playing tricks with texture. Curvy objects may look soft and squishy, but Starck's inviting chaise longue is made of hard, polished metal.

METAL BEATER

Israeli-born Ron Arad (*b.*1951) trained as an architect, but began to design furniture in the '80s for his London shop, One-Off. His early works were mainly in metal and concrete, and included shelving systems built from Kee Klamp (industrial scaffolding pieces). Bringing scaffolding into the home was unusual but supremely practical – shelf heights could be adjusted as the user's requirements evolved.

REINVENTING THE WHEEL

Arad became known for his unconventional forms. Storage systems of the 1990s included the Bookworm bookcase ('92), for which he bent one long piece of metal into a surreal shape. Arad's RTW bookcase ('96) was a triumph of technology. Its free-spinning outer wheel allowed the RTW to be rolled from one end of the room to the other. The shelves were locked within the wheel and were always the right way up, even when the bookcase was moving!

Arad's Bookworm (above, '92) played on the term for a book-lover – it was in the shape of a long, wriggly worm! Riveted metal 'books' made the book-ends. Books on Arad's RTW (left, '96) always stayed level, thanks to its revolutionary design.

DIY FURNITURE DESIGN

Ron Arad's collaboration with the British design company Inflate led to the Memo chair. The idea was that you sat in the chair and used a vacuum cleaner to suck out any excess air from the chair. The result was a chair that was moulded to fit exactly the contours of your body – a unique piece of tailor-made furniture. Part of the fun was that the user played a part in creating the final product.

Any vacuum cleaner would do, but the bagless Dyson Dual Cyclone was the only one as unconventional as the Memo chair!

INTERIORS

Sophisticated consumers demanded stylish leisure venues. To attract cool customers, hotels and public spaces employed star designers to give their interiors a makeover.

MIX AND MATCH

The one designer who had managed to achieve pop star status was French-born Philippe Starck. He styled interiors in every major city of the world. Starck's inventiveness lay in his ability to mix unusual materials and textures. For the Asahi Super Dry Hall, Tokyo (1989), he used lush, maroon velvet padded walls with gold tasselling for a new romantic look. He used padded walls again for the Felix Discotheque, Hong Kong ('93), but this time the effect was of a drinking den on a space station! The textured glass tables were lit from within and rose from the floor like sculptures.

Starck's design for the Peninsula Hotel included the space-age Felix Discotheque, on the 29th floor. It had eerie lighting and lime-green walls.

Philippe Starck (b.1949)

STARCK FACTS

Philippe Starck first trained as an architect, but achieved worldwide fame with designs that include toothbrushes, kettles, chairs and whole buildings. Much of his work is said to be biomorphic, which means that the objects imitate the appearance of living things.

Starck pays attention to every last detail. Taps in the Peninsula Hotel are designed in organic, twisted metal.

INSPIRATIONAL INTERIOR

The revival of raw, industrial materials such as metal and concrete had begun in the 1980s. Known as high tech, this style was embodied in Ron Arad's work. He was also involved in softening the look.

Ron Arad's interior for London restaurant Belgo Noord ('94) displayed his signature curves. Metal sat beside wood, black mixed with neutral shades.

Arad's most influential interior was the New Tel Aviv Opera House: its style was copied by many designers in the '90s. The interior had no fussy ornamentation or pictures cluttering the clean, white walls. However, it was far from stark. The walls may have been bare, but they curved, with organic holes that allowed a clever play of soft light. Such simplicity provided the perfect backdrop for the glittering bronze staircase.

The centrepiece of Tel Aviv's Opera House foyer ('88) was its stunning staircase in beaten bronze. Natural, sunshine tones were widely imitated in the '90s.

For his studio and furniture showroom, Arad converted a derelict warehouse ('91). The office space was covered in a PVC skin stretched over a steel shell.

ARCHITECTURE

Post-modern architects had more new materials to play with than ever before.

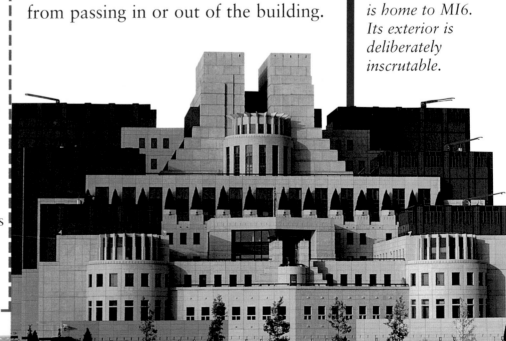

An aerial view of Gehry's Guggenheim Museum in Bilbao, Spain, completed in '97.

COMPLEX BUILDINGS

American Frank Gehry (*b*.1929) was one of the most imaginative architects of the age. His creations broke all the rules – he even built a restaurant shaped like a fish! Rather than creating huge monoliths, Gehry clustered together smaller units, giving the appearance of a sprouting, organic object. This is seen in his designs for the Guggenheim Museum in Bilbao, Spain and the Frederick R Weisman Art Museum in Minneapolis, United States.

Kansai International Airport ('95).

FEAT OF ENGINEERING

With land at a premium in Japan, the architect in charge of the new airport headed out to sea. Italian Renzo Piano (*b*.1937) built Kansai International Airport on a man-made island in Osaka Bay that is linked to the mainland by a 3-km long bridge. The sea cushions the building in an earthquake. The architecture is as stunning as the engineering. He gave the airport a high-tech roof of 1.7 km of undulating glass and steel.

BUILT-IN TECHNOLOGY

British architect Terry Farrell (*b*.1940) came up with a suitably forbidding style of architecture for the new headquarters for the British secret service. Vauxhall Cross ('93) is perfectly symmetrical and decorated with alarming spikes. The concrete walls even have a built-in mesh that stops electro-magnetic information from passing in or out of the building.

Vauxhall Cross is home to MI6. Its exterior is deliberately inscrutable.

20

Shining titanium walls, complete with brick-like texture, emphasise the crazy curves of Gehry's building. They create distorted reflections, echoing the museum's industrial location and the nearby sea.

The Getty Center, Los Angeles, is like a mini-city dedicated to art and culture. There are pavilions, cafes, restaurants, gardens and galleries. It was designed by Richard Meier (b.1934) and completed in '97.

The imposing, zigzagged structure of the Jewish Museum has been compared to a lightning bolt. The walls are covered in zinc.

MUSEUM MEMORIAL

Completed in 1999, the Jewish Museum in Berlin, Germany, is an example of how architecture can put forward a powerful message. The architect, Daniel Libeskind (b.1946), planned the museum around a central space or void. This emptiness was a reminder of Berlin's missing Jews, who either fled Nazi Germany or died in concentration camps. It also reminds us that what an architect leaves out can be as important as what he or she puts in.

MIGHTY MONUMENTS

The 20th century drew to a close with a flurry of building. These structures celebrated the present and looked forward to the future, with the same sense of optimism as post-war skyscrapers, such as the Seagram Building.

TECHNOLOGY ON DISPLAY

One style of architecture that made a feature of technology was the industrial look. British architect Richard Rogers (*b.*1933) was known for his futuristic approach. He designed the Pompidou Centre, Paris ('77) in collaboration with Renzo Piano and the Lloyd's Building, London ('86). Both projects showed off the struts, girders and other workings that architects usually hide. The beauty of Rogers' Millennium Dome, at Greenwich, London, was its proud display of how it was constucted. The 12 steel masts supporting its Teflon-coated glass-fibre 'skin' rose 100 metres into the sky and were painted an eye-catching orange.

The Haas Haus ('90) in Vienna was designed by Hans Hollein (b.1934). The mix of stone veneer and glass reflected the city's history and future. Inside, it had a stunning, celestial ceiling (top).

The 'skin' of London's Millenium Dome has a lifespan of about 50 years. The Dome's many critics felt annoyed that £750 million had been spent on a 'temporary' building (left and above).

TOWERING GIANT

During the '80s, the economies of Southeast Asia exploded and countries raced to build prestigious skyscrapers. Argentine-born architect Cesar Pelli (*b.*1926) designed a uniquely Malay building. Completed in autumn 1997, the 88-storey Petronas Towers overtook the Sears Tower's 22-year record as the world's tallest office block, topping 450 metres. The interior was decorated in local materials and included a prayer room for Muslim workers; the symmetrical exterior drew on the intricate, geometric patterns of Islamic art, and was topped with 73.5-metre high pinnacles. The building's record-breaking height was achieved thanks to 16 columns at the base of each tower.

A unique sky bridge links the twin towers at the 42nd storey, giving steadying support. The bridge makes Petronas Towers look rather like a gateway. In fact, the building forms a showy entrance to the newly-developed 'Golden Triangle' business district of Kuala Lumpur, Malaysia.

Cesar Pelli designed Britain's tallest building, Canary Wharf Tower ('91). The 50-storey obelisk is 243.8 m high. It was the first skyscraper to be clad in stainless steel – 16,000 pieces of it!

DESIGNS ON WHEELS

Transport design focuses more on safety and performance initially, but a trend for 'friendly' design hit the roads in the late 1990s.

The Volkswagen Beetle was relaunched in '98.

TOYS FOR GROWN-UPS

City-dwellers turned to bikes and scooters in an attempt to avoid urban congestion. In contrast to the aggressive models of the 1970s, bikes had rounded styling that appealed to men and women alike. At the same time, toy-like micro-cars appeared, such as Ford's curvy Ka. The classic VW Beetle built up its playful reputation in the *Herbie* films. In '98, the Beetle was updated. The new model kept the lovable, face-like front of the original, but was more streamlined and easier to handle.

Bike or car? BMW blurs the boundaries with the weather-proof C1. Its tubular aluminium frame has built-in crumple zones to protect a rider in a crash.

The latest cars feature a built-in navigator. The satellite-linked routeplanner helps drivers to plan their quickest route and to avoid any traffic jams.

THE QUEST FOR SPEED

The official one-mile (1.6-km) land speed record is held by British driver Andy Green in his car *Thrust SSC*. In October '97, Green drove the car faster than the speed of sound in Nevada, USA. The car is powered by two aircraft-style Rolls-Royce jet engines, which generate 22,680 kg of thrust. Sound travels at 331.29 m/sec (about 1193 km/h) and *Thrust SSC* was the first car in history to break the sound barrier.

As more cars fill up the roads, especially in city centres, it becomes harder to find a parking space. Renault's prototype for an energy-efficient electric micro-car, the Matra Zoom, solves this problem. It is already compact, but makes itself smaller for parking by tucking its back wheels under its body!

The Japanese Nozomi super-express (left) is the fastest of the bullet trains, cruising at 300 km/h. The Hikari (on the right) is slightly slower.

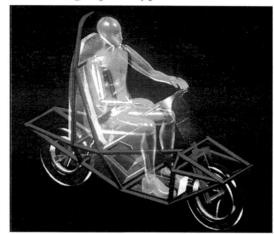
TOP TRAINS

The record for the fastest train journey time is held by the Japanese bullet train Nozomi 500. Its super-sharp nose cuts through the air at an average speed of 261.8 km/h. Japanese bullet trains, known as shinkansen, run on continuously-welded lines. This has put a stop to the old-fashioned 'clickety-clack' of wheels bumping over the joins in the track. The fastest European train is the French TGV (Train à grand vitesse). At 254.3 km/h, its fastest average journey time is slower than the Nozomi's, but in 1990 TGV Atlantique hit a record-breaking top speed of 515.3 km/h.

Thrust SSC topped 1,225 km/h in the Nevada Desert ('97).

The Anglo-French Eurostar ('94) travels at 300 km/h.

GOING GREEN

Environmental concerns had been raised in the 1980s. By the '90s, they had trickled into mainstream design. Designers began to use recycled and recyclable materials. They tried to create products that would be kind to the environment and that would not use too much precious energy.

RECYCLED CLOTHES

Green concerns have led to the development of eco-friendly fabrics. Tencel is a strong, stretchy fabric made from wood pulp gathered from sustainable forests. The synthetic fleece Polartec is made from recycled plastic bottles.

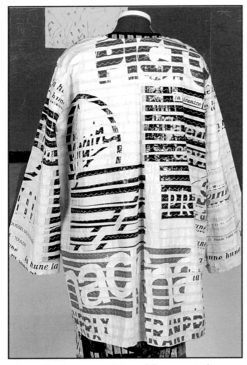

French designer Myrold creates haute couture dresses and coats from used plastic bags.

WIND-UP MERCHANT

British inventor Trevor Baylis (*b.*1937) invented the wind-up radio in '93 with the developing world in mind. People in remote parts of Africa were not receiving safety information about disease or war because they could not afford batteries for a radio. Baylis' Freeplay radio had three power sources: a spring, for winding up, a rechargeable battery, and solar panels. Baylis also invented a wind-up torch.

Boats returned to sail power to cut costs and conserve fuel. With less fuel to carry, ship designs could become more streamlined.

26

A million tonnes of vehicle exhaust gases are emitted each year in London alone. One green solution to inner city pollution was the pedicab, which does not burn any fuel at all. It was based on the Japanese rickshaw and ran on pedal-power.

The Smart was a collaboration between Mercedes-Benz and Swatch. At 2.5 m long, the two-seater was small and energy efficient – the perfect car for space-conscious city-dwellers!

Proving that sensible technology can look good, the Freeplay range comes in fashionable plastics: choose from solid yellow or black, or go for transparent blue, red or green.

AIR POLLUTION

Cars are one of the chief causes of air pollution. As fuel burns in a car's engine, harmful gases are emitted from the car's exhaust. Measures to combat this have included the introduction of catalytic converters and lead-free petrol, and trials of alternative fuels, including electricity, solar power and biogas.

During the 1980s, big cars were status symbols, but in the '90s smaller, more fuel-efficient models became acceptable to consumers. Some people even left their cars at home and opted for public transport or pedal-power in the form of push-bikes and pedicabs.

WHAT A LOAD OF RUBBISH

After decades of throwaway culture, the public learnt to recycle, and began to sort their newspapers and bottles into different bins. Products such as washing powders and liquids became available in refill packs to minimise on wasteful packaging. Newspapers switched to recycled paper. New fabrics appeared that were created from yesterday's rubbish – Polartec, for example, was a soft, fleecy fabric manufactured from old plastic bottles. Even car makers took note. The BMW 3 series made a feature of its eco-awareness. Parts of the bodywork were moulded from recycled plastics (*shown in green*). Almost all of the rest of its body was made from recyclable plastics (*shown in blue*).

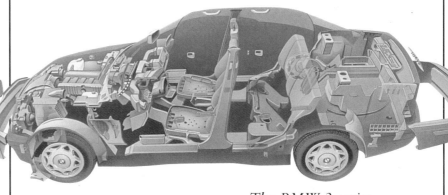

The BMW 3 series

VIRTUALLY REAL

The 1990s saw huge leaps in the power of computers, which made it possible for them to create very lifelike models of the world. Instead of staring at a flat picture on a computer screen, it was now possible to put on a virtual reality (VR) suit, and climb inside the picture.

Pop stars and advertisers used computers to make their products more fun. Björk was morphed to become an animal in the video to her song, Hunter ('97).

Scientists can use virtual reality to test ideas. Here a young scientist builds new molecules by hand.

LIKE REALITY, ONLY BETTER

VR had all sorts of uses, though it was used mainly for exciting new video games at first. Nuclear explosions could be modelled on computer, for example, instead of carrying out nuclear tests.

THROUGH THE LOOKING GLASS

Virtual reality works by linking your body to a computer via sensors. The computer senses when you move, and calculates your new position, including your new view of the space. You feel that you are 'in' the picture that the computer is creating. Advanced versions include little machines in the gloves and boots, which resist when you press – if you reach out to grab a virtual object, the glove actively pushes against your fingers as you 'touch' the object, rather than letting your hand pass through it.

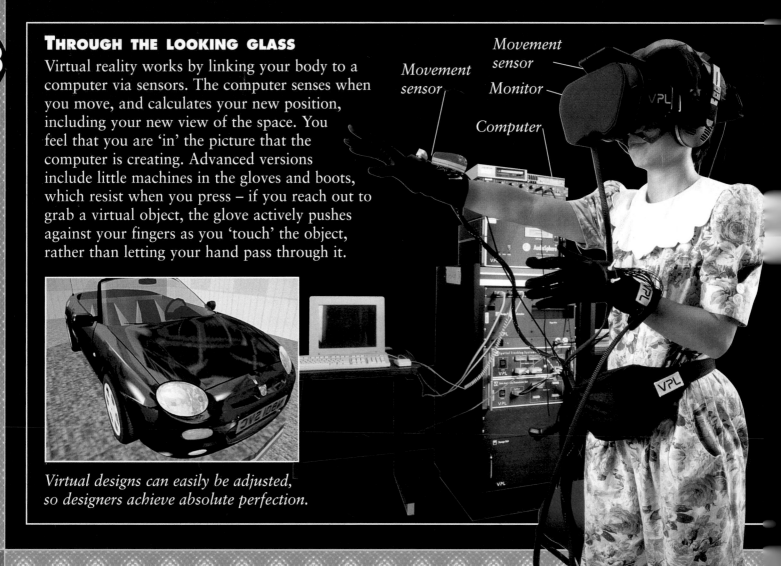

Movement sensor

Movement sensor

Movement sensor

Monitor

Computer

Virtual designs can easily be adjusted, so designers achieve absolute perfection.

On the cover of Björk's album, Homogenic *('97), designers Me Company used state-of-the-art computers to reshape the singer, creating extraordinary eyes, hair, nails and clothing.*

For countries with a car pollution problem, VR offered the prospect of virtual offices – commuters could stay at home, put on a headset, and 'telecommute' to work.

VIRTUAL DANGER

There was a scary side to virtual reality, as well. In the film, *The Matrix* ('99), nasty machines used virtual reality to keep people under control.

Kyoko Date ('96) was the first virtual superstar. Designed by HoriPro to be every teenager's dream date, Kyoko Date was a computer-generated 16-year-old pop star, with a huge following in Japan.

GENERATION NEXT

Virtual reality technology might have other benefits – and pitfalls. The film *Lawnmower Man* ('92) explored what might happen if VR was used to help people overcome learning difficulties. Although the film had a nasty ending, it made people realise that new generations growing up with VR technology would see and feel things that adults before them had never experienced. Would the gap between adults and children grow as more of young people's lives were spent in 'cyberspace'? Would children learn faster and become more clever than their parents?

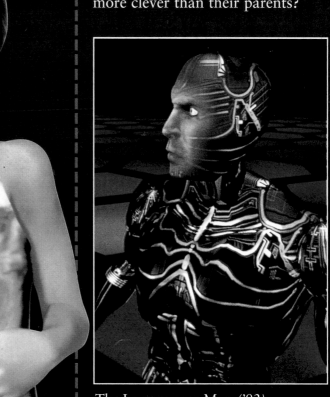

The Lawnmower Man ('92)

GLOSSARY

ANALOGUE A system of storing and carrying information using gradual changes in a continuous signal.

ANDROGYNOUS Combining male and female qualities.

BIOGAS A fuel made from natural rotted matter, such as plant waste or sewage.

BIOMORPHIC Describes an object that resembles a living thing.

DIGITAL A system of storing and carrying information using a code of On (1) and Off (0).

HIGH-TECH In architecture and design, a style that celebrates technology. 'High-tech' can also mean the use of advanced materials or equipment.

INTERNET Links which connect computer networks together creating a global network.

MODERNISM A cultural trend that emerged in the early 20th century. Rejecting fussy decoration, modernists believed that the appearance of an object or building should be determined by its use.

MONOLITH A massive, uniform block, such as a stone at Stonehenge, or a skyscraper.

OBELISK A tall, four-sided, tapering pillar, topped with a pyramid.

PEDICAB A cross between a rickshaw and a tricycle, used as a green alternative to the taxi in some big cities.

POP ART Art that draws inspiration from consumerism and popular culture.

POST-MODERNISM A cultural trend that emerged in the 1960s and '70s in reaction to modernism. It took a playful, pick-and-mix approach to the styles of the past.

PROTOTYPE A test model for a new product.

TEFLON Trademarked name for a non-stick graphite-based material.

TITANIUM A lightweight, strong metal which is resistant to corrosion (wearing away by air, water or chemicals).

VIRTUAL REALITY A computer simulation of an environment the user can enter.

WORLD WIDE WEB Network, or web, of information published on pages and accessed through the internet.

DESIGN HIGHLIGHTS

- *Philippe Starck for Alessi: Juicy Salif*
- *Gaultier designs costumes for Madonna*
- *Hollein: Haas Haus*

19

- *Ralph Erskine: the London Ark*
- *Pelli: Canary Wharf Tower*

19

- *Gehry: Powerplay armchair*

19

- *Starck: Peninsula Hotel* •*Alessi: Family Follows Fiction range*
- *Terry Farrell: Vauxhall Cross*
- *Alessi: Anna G corkscrew*

19

- *Inflate founded*
- *Westwood: Vive la Cocotte collection*
- *Piano: Kansai International Airport*
- *Arad: RTW bookcase*
- *Nikon E2 digital camera*
- *Philips Web TV*

19

- *Arad: Fantastic Plastic Elastic chair* •*Gehry: Guggenheim, Bilbao*
- *Meier: Getty Center*
- *Pelli: Petronas Towers*
- *Apple: iMac*
- *'New' VW Beetle*
- *Alessi: Folpo*

19

- *Rogers: Millennium Dome* •*Libeskind: Jewish Museum, Berlin*
- *Smart car*

19

TIMELINE

	WORLD EVENTS	TECHNOLOGY	FAMOUS PEOPLE	ART & MEDIA
90	•Iraq invades Kuwait: Gulf War begins	•Launch of Hubble Space Telescope •TGV Atlantique *hits* 515.3 km/h	•Nelson Mandela freed in South Africa •Death of artist Keith Haring	•The Simpsons •*Bassomatic*: Set the Controls for the Heart of the Bass •*Jeunet/Caro*: Delicatessen
91	•Break up of USSR		•Yeltzin is Russian leader •Aung San Suu Kyi wins Nobel Peace Prize •Calvin Klein signs up Kate Moss for $2 million	•*Jostein Gaarder*: Sophie's World •*Douglas Coupland*: Generation X •*Katsuhiro Otomo*: Akira
92	•Australia drops oath of loyalty to British monarch	•*Philips Digital Compact Cassette (DCC)*	•Warhol's Marilyn x 100 sells for $3.4 million	•*Koons*: Puppy •*Brian Eno*: Nerve Net •*Prince*: Love Symbol Album •*Jungle music is born*
93	•PLO & Israel sign peace agreement	•*Apple Newton* •*Casio Alti-Thermo watch*	•Bill Clinton becomes US President	•*Spielberg*: Jurassic Park •*Björk*: Debut •*E Annie Proulx*: The Shipping News •*Tim Burton*: The Nightmare before Christmas
94	•South Africa: Mandela is first black president •Civil war in Rwanda	•*Channel Tunnel completed* •*Genetically-modified tomatoes go on sale*	•Kurt Cobain commits suicide	•*Tarantino*: Pulp Fiction •*Damien Hirst*: Away from the Flock •*Helen Chadwick*: effluvia •*Irvine Welsh*: Trainspotting
95	•Terrorist bomb, Oklahoma, USA •Kobe earthquake •Nerve gas attacks in Tokyo by Aum Shinrikyo cult	•*Baylis: Freeplay wind-up radio*	•Assassination of Israeli PM Yitzak Rabin •OJ Simpson acquitted in murder trial	•Tank Girl •*Christo wraps the Reichstag* •*The Prodigy*: Music for the Jilted Generation •*Seamus Heaney wins Nobel Prize*
96	•'Mad Cow' disease: bans on British beef	•*Sony PlayStation launched* •*Prototype stealth ship, Sea Wraith (UK)*	•Death of artist Helen Chadwick •Tombraider star Lara Croft is born •Death of Francois Mitterand	•*Disney*: Toy Story •*Spice Girls*: Spice •*John Pawson*: Minimum •*Orange Prize for Fiction launched*
97	•UK returns Hong Kong to China •Roswell report denies alien encounter •Blair is UK PM	•*Dolly the Sheep* •Thrust SSC breaks sound barrier •*Sojourner Rover on Mars* •*Bandai: Tamagotchi* •*Apple: eMate*	•IBM's Deep Blue *beats* Kasparov at chess •Death of Princess Diana •Versace shot •Boerge Ousland crosses Antarctica alone	•*Alex Garland*: The Beach •*Elton John re-masters Candle in the Wind in response to death of Diana, Princess of Wales*
98	•South Africa: Truth & Reconciliation Report •Birth of the euro	•*International Space Station: construction begins* •First vertical-drop theme park ride: Oblivion •*Digital Versatile Disc (DVD)*	•Death of Frank Sinatra •Death of Japanese director Akira Kurosawa •Death of animal rights activist Linda McCartney	•*Anish Kapoor exhibition* •*Talvin Singh*: ok •*Ted Hughes*: Birthday Letters
99	•NATO troops in air strikes on Yugoslavia •Nuclear testing crisis, India & Pakistan	•*Zanussi: Zoe washing machine, Oz refrigerator & Teo cooker*	•Madonna is face of Max Factor •Prince Edward marries Sophie Rhys-Jones	•*Lucas*: Episode 1: The Phantom Menace •*Philip Glass*: Dracula •Pokemon

INDEX